Fiverr

Actionable Tips to Earn More, Attract Clients and Love What You Do

(How to Become a Trusted Fiverr Seller Who Regularly Earns)

Nick Brinson

Published By **Ryan Princeton**

Nick Brinson

All Rights Reserved

Fiverr: Actionable Tips to Earn More, Attract Clients and Love What You Do (How to Become a Trusted Fiverr Seller Who Regularly Earns)

ISBN   978-1-77485-664-2

Legal & Disclaimer

TABLE OF CONTENTS

Introduction

As you're reading this book this moment, I'd say that you're a novice freelancer with no experience or the skills you have (that you are aware of) to provide.

So , how can you make money online with these two things?

How can you become a successful freelancer, who is payed for the work you do?

In this quick guide, I'll explain the route you can follow to earn a full-time living using Fiverr.

I'll help you understand the most effective types of services you can provide today. I'll help you become proficient in your chosen area of expertise or category. I'll assist you in setting up your account in a proper way. I'll help you create a listing that can be converted. In addition I'll teach you how to make 2-3x more cash by introducing customers to your other products.

I am of the opinion that anyone can accomplish this.

Anyone who is willing to do the work can be successful as a freelancer. You can work from home and never have to have to worry about two-hour commutes for a second.

Can it be done?

It's probably but not.

Do you expect to earn six figures in one year?

I don't know However, it's possible.

I can't guarantee anything.

The results you will get will depend on your personal preferences.

In addition, how much time will you invest?

The first two weeks will prove to be most challenging.

Once you're proficient in your chosen field and are able to market your services it becomes much easy and you'll begin earning more money, with much less effort.

Let's jump right in and get started.

Chapter 1: Getting Started

Within this segment, you will learn how to start and how long it will take to build a great profile and get a gig on Fiverr How to motivate yourself to keep going and which services to choose.

The services you choose are the most crucial element of the whole procedure, since they determine the extent to which you earn money.

I'll go over ways to come up with ideasthat will yield more profit, how to study and beat your competition and also what type of job you should be doing.

Let's get going!

How to make it happen

One of the questions I get asked frequently is "How do I get to be at Fiverr for full time?" It all depends on how much time you put with the site, your ongoing advancement of your work and how happy your customers will be.

Fiverr offers an internet-based marketplace that offers freelance services. The site is designed that allows freelancers to provide services to buyers around the world. The company lets buyers make payments in advance to "gigs," which are any kind of freelance service including web design, music recording and social media marketing copywriting, and much more. When Fiverr first came out the service, each gig was initially priced at just five dollars however now, sellers can choose to charge more or provide various types of services.

The first thing you need to make on Fiverr is to create your profile and your first job. It is then necessary to use the platform to gain knowledge about your clients and your company.

I recommend you spend an afternoon off to begin using the platform, and be aware of every particular. The more thorough your profile and job description is, the more professional you appear professional. You'll also need be aware of the amount of time you'll use the website. For instance, I'm spending approximately half of my working time using the site every morning (to work, respond to customers, make contact and promote my work, develop my offerings, or gain feedback from my colleagues).

One of the primary tasks you'll need to complete is set aside certain time. Choose the length of time you'll be active on the platform in order to plan and prepare your potential customers. Some people claim that they'd love to join Fiverr and have been there for a long time but aren't sure what's wrong, or do not know what they should write on their profile or gig. I look over their services and see that they offer a one-sentence description, and make their customers wait for ages to get a response, and are only on the site only once per year and don't finish their orders in time. Sometimes, they do not even have a portfolio that showcases their offerings!

It is essential to be specific and specific. Set your ultimate goals and work to reach them. When you begin taking actions on your freelance path it will be much easier to go on.

Imagine if, after one month, you create your Fiverr account and earn money at your home. If you don't start and you don't succeed, you'll never make it. The longer you wait to get started the more money you'll be making every day be lost. Every day you miss a paycheck, even when it's only 15 dollars per day. If you wait the course of a month, it could be more than 450 dollars and completely gone. So, I'd suggest that you block out the time you have on your calendar and set goals, reward yourself and get started on your journey on Fiverr.

Selecting the best service

It is by far the most crucial aspect of creating a gig with Fiverr. Be sure to select an option that is financially profitable instead of one that is okay. Otherwise you'll waste valuable time in creating and promoting. I've learned this hard-way many of my projects have turned out to be complete failures. Sure, some have had great success and I've learnt lots about what kinds of services and categories are a success and which aren't, as well as how you should be thinking about the process.

In the beginning, you must consider all you can offer in a way of service such as your current and former job, your hobbies, what you're passionate about, cities that you've lived in or studied, languages you're familiar with or things your friends might ask for information about (just like "Oh please tell me more about this," as well as "How did you come to this profession?" ?"), and what do you're involved in often.

Perhaps, for instance, you work as a receptionist. That implies you will have phone conversations and you can type, copy or take notes and transcribe or translate. You may have to deal with challenging individuals, Overcome changes within your company or face issues in workplace political issues.

Anything you might think of is an interesting service.

Another example: what videos you stream on YouTube or the books you've read, or any other topic you're fascinated by - make an extensive list. It'll be a long list of subjects and actions related to these topics. Keep it in mind, as it can be helpful when developing your service and also for the keywords to include in your.

It is usually when people consider "Oh good, I'm familiar with this and I'll just do the simplest task." But here's the crucial part that you should not let it go. You must think about what you can expect to be paid for, not what seems simple for you to do.

One of my less than successful performances was "I will make violin karaoke tracks for the song you select." The thought was that that was a great deal because a lot of people enjoy the music of the violin and karaoke for singing or playing with. But, if someone's searching for music backing tracks you can be sure they'll seek it out via Google or YouTube instead of Fiverr. Additionally, these customers might not be the best type of person, since they may want to pay less since they're not experts. They weren't exactly the right people to use Fiverr to help me with my failed job. To purchase a service from this site, users must have a genuine need to solve their issue and feel that it's worth investing their money into.

You must be thinking about whether this is something that I'd want to be willing to pay for?

One of the most common misconceptions regarding Fiverr can be that freelancing freelancers just create a fiver because they show the lowest cost. This is completely false. Additionals and other types of services will always raise prices for the basic package. The typical low cost is for something that you'd take less than ten minutes to complete. As an example, my standard cost is 15 seconds of recording a violin. This means I have to invest under five minutes recording. Most of the time, this isn't enough time for composers or producers who require violin recordings. They have to pay for the entire package or purchasing various or more expensive packages to receive the quality they're hoping for.

It is important to select one that's a bit of special, so that there isn't too much competition (and there are lots of competition on Fiverr currently) However, it's essential to pick something that's broad enough that lots of customers will purchase it.

This means that you need to consider who your clients are If they're on Fiverr and also how many are using the site. If you're not sure consider looking at the the Internet. It's a great sign that you've found guides or books on the product you'd like to sell, or if you find other businesses that are offering the same type of service that you'd like to offer anyone who is already paying for is a great indicator.

How can you beat your competition?
Once you've got an enormous list of suggestions for your service Take a review of Fiverr to figure out which you should go after. You must look at what competition is available on the website: lots of generally well-known general gigs are available on Fiverr The trick is to focus with a clear service.
Start by logging onto the platform and enter the services you'd like to provide. Test a variety of variants of the search using various keywords to ensure that you can spot the gaps between different kinds of. For instance, for the Recording Violin gig, I

tried searching for "Violinist string quartet recording violinist and session musician, as well as session violin" and so on.

Ideally, you'll see at minimum three or two pages of results, and the top performers have 100-200 reviews.

If there's only few gigs available that you're looking for and only some reviews, you're likely to be too narrow of a segment. There is a good chance that those users aren't making any revenue, which means it's not worthwhile on Fiverr. However If search results cover longer than 15 pages, and the entire front page is filled with users with over 500 reviews The market is packed, and it'll be difficult in order to be on the first page, unless you have an enormous number of subscribers or fans, or a large mailing list (they might help you with your first order and help more sales). If, however, you're like me and just starting out, it's likely to be a bit crowded already.

If you do locate the perfect services following the earlier guidelines Take a look through the top gigs. perhaps their services are not up-to-date or too general. Their reviews aren't the most impressive or their portfolio might be of poor quality. Find out what isn't right in their service and how you can stand out. It's likely that many of them won't relate to keywords you entered. Perhaps they're difficult to comprehend or you've got more experience, could create a more compelling description, upload an attractive thumbnail, possess a more professional portfolio and other things. This could be the deciding factor in a client's decision to choose over other options that are listed.

Chapter 2: Organizing Your Gigs

This section will be talking about how to plan your gigs, what you could realistically earn (based upon my experiences with Fiverr, with various gigs that generated various sums of money) as well as the specific and actual craft that you'll need to perform, the timings pricing, quality, and prices in general the most frequent concerns I receive from my clients.

I will also guide you know the process behind the scenes of how I design my shows and then analyze what your expectations should be.

How much will you earn?
Many people will be angry at me for this statement However, the truth is that it is a matter of fact!

I'll give you the most detailed information I can regarding the amount of money my gigs have earned and a quick step-by step guide to help you determine where the cash might be.

The products that are purchased most often are business and marketing-related gigs which help people earn more money. People are happy to invest money in anything that makes money since it is a genuine investment for them. It all depends on the professionalism of the worker and quality, however gigs like those can earn as much as 4000 or 5000 dollars each month. Naturally, some reputable Fiverr sellers earn much more, but this is merely a guideline.

My recording studio for violins has been generating approximately 900 dollars per month, over a period of one year of growth. There are several pauses in my business due to travel and performances. Keep in mind that these numbers are not absolute and you may be more efficient and make more income by taking the correct steps.

Fiverr will take 20% of the revenue that you earn, which means you need to factor the amount into your cost. The website promotes your company and also showcases your service to potential customers, so it's a reasonable amount when you consider. Make sure you are valuing yourself properly and evaluate the options for what type of service you'd like to provide to customers with care. Make your choices based on the likelihood that they'll be sufficient to make enough money to pay for the time you'll invest on the site.

Unexpected expenses and income

There's a slight loss of currency exchange as the website only works in dollars. So regardless of whether you'll need to convert your money into euros, pounds or any other currency, there'll be an occasional difference in the amount of money you earn. I recommend that you transfer your the money to a bank that has a low exchange rate (such as Transferwise or Revolut).

One thing one way to boost your earnings is to market the services you offer on different websites that offer freelance services (Upwork, Peopleperhour, etc.). Sincerely there's been no other website that has even come close to the Fiverr revenue however, it's worthwhile to boost your earnings. I'm probably earning about a few hundred dollars per year from other sites, so it's always worth it to try.

What is the time frame for delivery?

I'd suggest that your service's cost (the most affordable, for example) is delivered within the range of one to three days. The less time you need in delivering, the faster the time frame for your gig to begin. You'll be able to add additional days of delivery when buyers request additional items within your offer. Personally, I believe that just one or two days are enough time to record 15 minutes of a track for a violin. If a customer is looking for an item on Fiverr typically, they want the fastest and most reliable one. The faster you can get and the better your chances of being selected. get selected at the beginning. After a while you'll be able to comprehend your schedule and adapt the schedule you have set. If you believe it will take longer, consider trying to divide the different phases of your process as to your service, so that you quickly earn more money and have more time to complete your task.

Do not worry too much about the precise amount of time needed to finish your project But remember that the perfect timing will give you more exposure on Fiverr. If you fail to deliver earlier than you expected customers could be unhappy, and may write a negative review. Take care when deciding on your timing settings. The faster you go the more Fiverr will present your profile to potential customers.

Other things you'll want to be aware of

It is possible add buzzwords to your descriptions. For instance, in my violin recording gig I ensure that I mention the terms "session musician professional violinist recording composer, arranger of strings" since that's what people are looking for. They're also going to look for in your resume and your profile.

Include a closing message in your letter to your customer. It is important to maintain contact with the customer. So, try to talk to them with them, asking them what they liked and what they didn'tlike, and what you can make to improve the quality of your service.

It's crucial to get feedback right from the beginning because it's an excellent method to make improvements and gain more sales.

Chapter 3: How To Create Your Gifts

This will be what's the "meat" part of the discussion. I'll walk you through step-by-step instructions on how to build your profile, the most successful gigs, the type of content and what do you write your content to grab the attention of potential customers as well as how do you upload or edit your profile your profile, and some tips and tricks that are hidden secrets of your Fiverr website.

Profile creation

Before you sell your product on Fiverr You'll have to set up your profile as a user. It is important to display your abilities, and also your abilities and education, qualifications as well as other certifications. This allows potential buyers to learn the more details about your skills and the qualifications you have to increase the trust they have in you.

The first step is to add your full name and profile photo. Your profile picture describes you and the service you'll offer to boost the trust of your customers.

Add a professional description/biography, using keywords that are related to the products you'll be selling to increase the likelihood of potential customers coming across your business. The more personable you appear the more trust you'll gain.

Complete the form with the information you've provided and add your qualifications appropriately: they could be connected to the products you'll offer Utilize the terms you had previously thought of when you chose the service you'd like to provide. You are able to include up to 15 different skills So make sure you are generous.

Make sure to verify and update all your social profiles - this will boost your credibility more.

When prospective buyers visit your page, they'll review everything they can to decide whether or not they should purchase your product. It's important to complete all details accurately.

Once you've completed this, you're prepared to launch your first business!

Designing a captivating title

The title is essential to draw attention of the buyer and create a memorable first impression.

In the beginning, you should make use of adjectives to describe your services. Many sellers claim they are professional however, if you include emotionality, your description makes a statement. For example the seller might provide the option of a "breathtaking" videos.

Add a related service. For example using video, you could add that you perform post-production.

Note the time of delivery: If you can deliver your service or product in less than 24 hours you should noting it in the name.

In the end, Fiverr recommends that you design your gig's title using keywords you would like people to discover you by. This will result in an SEO-friendly URL that is great for SEO and onsite searches. After you've saved your job, you can go back and alter the title using the above tips.

Subcategories and tags

Choose your gig category, taking into consideration your services. Fiverr will then suggest subcategories that match your preferences However, use your sense and pick the category in which you will be able to compete successfully against other sellers in a smart way.

When you're there, choose your gig's metadata. These are additional filtering options available for your gig. The more specific you are about your keywords more potential customers will be able to find your gig.

Then, add the tags that you recognize with the greatest. You may choose as many as five tags.

Be aware that subcategories and tags, metadata and subcategories will be displayed as options to filter buyers, so be sure to choose your filters carefully.

What is the best price to charge?

If you're starting on Fiverr do not focus excessively on your base price of your gig. The real earnings are in the additional services. The base price, the one that you see on every gig listed on the page of search (for example, in the vicinity of where the company's name is) is merely an attempt to get the attention of the client.

It is important that you establish a fair price.

Utilizing three different packages within your Fiverr service could boost your the amount of money you earn by 64%, which is definitely worth the effort.

A great example of an additional service is the way I got started using the platform. My initial price was $5 dollars to record 15 minutes of violin recording. If the customer desired more time or a faster delivery, they would have to purchase an additional gig and thus pay more.

You can use items that you sell for more like:
* Revisions to the original
* Extra-fast delivery
• More time with the service
* More micro-services
One way to be honest with the buyer is to make sure to communicate in chat all the additional services you provide; they might think about buying more than were expecting. Get as much detail as possible about your customer's is looking for and wants during the chat so that you can understand it and suggest things you can add to your offer.

In general, it's best to start with basic rates and services, such as my 15-second recording of the violin. It is evident that customers request more or have a discussion with you. If they do purchase the basic package that they are buying, it has to require only a small amount of effort and time from your side; therefore the price should be reasonable for you and your customer.

What do you need to write?

The next step to create an effective Fiverr job is to write a description of your gig that inspires people to buy. There's plenty of space to write and here's what you must do:

• Highlight the benefits to customers, and how your service will assist them to achieve success or get business.

Tell them why you're best person to be working with. Five-star-rated sellers with thousands of satisfied customers typically starts with this as it helps convince prospective buyers that they're picking the right company. It is important to clearly define what is included in the service you provide.

Include social proof links--if you have external proof that makes your services look professional then this is the best location to display it.

If you're unsure of what to include take a look at the top competitors you've studied earlier and look over their descriptions. Then , you can modify them and add your own personal details to make a compelling description for your job.

The next section should you should inform your customers what you'll require from them in order to complete the order. For instance for those who are creating your logo, you'll need to be aware of the company's brand. Likewise, if you're creating content, they'll need to supply information on their target audience. If you're recording tracks for guitar it's necessary to have the mp3, tempo and chords.

Interacting with customers

After you have completed your professional portfolio, and creating your business, the most important aspect of your work with Fiverr involves dealing with clients. Whatever you offer and wherever you're sharing your gigs at the end of your day, you need to present yourself and engage in conversations with your customers. If you don't succeed it is impossible to earn any product or service after all your hard work as well as your research.

The first step is to learn ENGLISH. This is the first step to effective communication.

Respond as quickly as you can. I recommend that you download the Fiverr application to your phone. Rapid responses make an excellent impression. the competition is doing it well. Buyers typically make contact with multiple sellers at once and the more responsive you respond, the greater chances you'll be able to get your job.

Use formal words: Common or casual expressions could offend anyone from a totally different society, so be cautious.

Try to sense what the customer wants through their words , and provide an authentic response. Don't give the impression as if you're giving an automated answer.

After you've completed your task and then deliver the item to the customer, you can leave a message in the attachment. Let them know what you're offering and the exact process you followed and ask if the customer is able to provide feedback on the quality of your service or product and then thank them for their purchase. The more polite and courteous you're the more likely the customer will be pleased with their experience and they'll be more inclined to give you a positive review.

Behind the scenes of the Fiverr website
It's important to have a thorough understanding of the sections on the site to understand the places where the different buttons are, and what you'll need. It's possible that this will change as time goes by however I'd like to show you how the interface appears like for me and how I utilize it. I've mentioned a range of subjects throughout this guide, such as making and editing gigs, as well as helping customers, and I'd like to make sure that you know how you accomplish those tasks.

It's the Fiverr.com homepage. You will check out the dashboard of my sellers here, which includes all the orders I have to complete and the ones I've delivered recently. It also shows the amount of each order as well as the status of each order.

If you click on the order button, you'll be able to view all the detailsof the order, including the buyer's requirements , information, along with the amount of duration of your leave. You can also add more time, talk to the buyer regarding concerns or other information you require, or utilize the resolution center if you're unable to reach the buyer.

This is where you can create and modify your gigs. This section is extremely beneficial for analytics, as it allows you to analyze changes that you may make to your gigs.

This page on analytics is among the most helpful. It provides a summary of your sales, orders as well as each sale and cancellations within a particular period of time - like the last 30 days, 3 months or the last year. It will help you understand the things you could be doing wrong and what you could make to improve the amount of sales you make.

The earnings page is where you are able to take your money out by transferring the money to your PayPal as well as your bank account (via Payoneer).

An effective way to get involved with Fiverr methods is to study the community. Plenty of informative posts about growing sales can be found on the forum or you can study on the "Learn" page that includes Professional Online courses that will provide you with badges for your profile (this increases your confidence).

It's an extremely easy to navigate website, with lots of possibilities, and simple to navigate (if you are fluent in English!).

Chapter 4: Final Touches

It's crucial to concentrate on specifics to attract customers' attention and establish trust.
The next section I will talk about the various finishing elements, including how to design an online portfolio that attracts buyers, a few SEO tricks to make it easy for the buyer, and also the best ways to promote your content and tips for thumbnails.

Making a portfolio that can be converted
Following the title and the price you've offered There's nothing more important then your resume. A professional portfolio can aid in attracting the clients you're looking for and get the interest of professionals who could enhance your career. It's an ongoing thing that

requires attention throughout your professional life on the web and should be something you put in a some time working on. It's your Fiverr CV, your business card or professional resume.

Include only your finest work. Quality over quantity is essential. Avoid feeling that you have to include everything you've ever done. It is also important to draw your ideal customers So keep this in mind when choosing your projects. For instance, if are looking to establish your name known as a rock artist it's not logical to put up Ed Sheeran acoustic covers you made ten years ago when you were learning guitar.

Flexibility: Make sure to mix your presentation so that all of your abilities are displayed. This could include personal projects or experiments that will help you get the kind of client that you've always wanted.

Utilize high-resolution photos and videos to showcase to your prospective clients the capabilities you have.

Get opinions, not just from your friends and family members who may not be telling the whole truth. Mentors, former colleagues and even trusted clients can provide valuable insight on how your portfolio is working for them.

SEO: Search Engine Optimization

Keywords are the foundation of your business. Through the use of keywords, you provide your clients a method to find your goal. This is where you have where you need to work hard. You can utilize a variety of tools such as LSI graphs, Kwfinder, and so on to find the right keywords that are relevant to your service on Fiverr.

The repetition of keywords in your gig's title descriptions, descriptions, and tags will increase your ranking on Fiverr. Also by creating a username using an expression or phrase that is associated with your skills will help promote the value of your gig to potential buyers. Repetition keywords in a way which is in your favor.

If you are targeting specific keywords for example, like "Instagram marketing"," it should be included in all of the title of your post, tag and the description (minimum three or two times in the description).

Video promo and thumbnail

You must make sure that you show what makes your business special. What is it that you offer customers an experience unlike any other you provide over others? Do you have a speedy delivery or your exceptional customer service? Make sure you write an appealing script prior to you begin recording or editing your video. Brainstorm. What would grab your attention If you were searching for a job like this?

Make sure to use upbeat, catchy tunes (or one that fits the speed of your video, your changes, the tone that you're trying to convey, etc.). Utilize font type and color to get the most LOOK-AT-MY GIG-FACTOR: attractive colors, large fonts, and crisp words.

Of course foremost, you must describe your gig. Make it appear as if your description of the gig does not exist (because some potential buyers will only see the promotional videos). In the short amount of time you've got to make your video What are the most important elements of your gig?

Chapter 5: Selling Out Your Services

Once you've learned how to build the ideal structure that is solid, you'll discover how to market your services in the following section. This section offers the most essential tips and specific actions you can take to boost your sales dramatically.

If you are able to get some momentum at the beginning, Fiverr can do the work for you. new customers will be able to passively call you daily.

How can I place my first Fiverr purchase?

There are some effective ways to get your very first purchase. One of the most successful is Fiverr's Buyer's Requests. This is an excellent feature

Fiverr offers, which is an excellent resource for novices who want to learn.

Buyers who are looking to purchase an item but are unable to locate the perfect gig will make a post on Fiverr's Requests, stating their needs. Buyers interested in selling will get in touch with an offer that is fair and you're sure to want to be among the buyers.

This is where you can take advantage. Offer your services at a lower cost than the competition.

You'll need to provide your services at a lower cost than other businesses to be successful on Fiverr. When you begin receiving more reviews and orders you are able to increase the price you charge, just as you've seen in the earlier sections.

For instance, customers could post an inquiry through Fiverr.

You can respond to these messages by messaging them. If you respond, be sure to clearly explain why you are more effective than other people as well as your price and your delivery time.

The customers might or may not call you If they do, it'll be simple to convince them using the right communications.

Early reviews and traction

One of the ways to get your gig on the right foot is getting reviews early. If you're successful it, you'll absolutely be blown away as more people will be able to see your work, you'll be mentioned as a possible suggestion under the most popular gigs, and it'll assist Fiverr ensure that your gig is a hit.

It is not allowed to purchase fake reviews on the website. They will not benefit you in the long term So, instead choose to increase your reviews naturally through providing a high-quality professional and reliable service.

I suggest that you create your account with professionalism and a memorable manner, maximizing it to draw the best customers. Inform your friends and family of your services. The majority of sellers do not discuss their work They only desire Fiverr to provide them with customers (that could be the reason the system doesn't show buyers the services offered by the newest sellers).

Promote your business, tell people about your services and invite people to leave reviews in case they appreciate the services you provide.

One thing I've found to be extremely helpful is to discover which area your prospective client is. For instance in the case of services for YouTubers who are just starting out (such as making an intro or graphic to YouTube channels) I'll search for small YouTubers' groups on Facebook and then join in their communities and send discounts or showcase my work on YouTube.

They can be asked for feedback. Some may be interested in purchasing your product or providing useful tips on how to make it effective.

I would suggest that you plan this type of promotion prior to when you launch your business on Fiverr and ensure you get people who are interested in your site the day you launch it.

Other methods to promote your events

As I've mentioned previously that the best strategy would be to use Facebook Groups.

You could also consider Facebook/Google/Instagram ads. It's

evident that this is a little more risky since you'll have to pay for advertisements. In this instance I recommend that you learn how to properly run Facebook advertisements through Fiverr Learn: the platform's classes are extremely efficient and useful.

You could also market the benefits of your Fiverr services by making podcasts, blog posts or YouTube videos as guests (with interviews regarding your products or other topics that relate to your professional activities) or, if it's an individual channel that you have created, include your link to your gig in the description, and also include your company's name in the video/blog post/talk. These are great ways to generate sales.

A great way to advertise your products is to trade things in exchange for an email address. This will build your mailing list and offer specials to those who are interested in your business. There's plenty of online information about creating this type of marketing. one of the most professional websites that offer this type services is Mailchimp.

I personally promote my services at least once every month, or once a month. I do this using Facebook and Instagram advertisements, as well as through my Instagram stories. I suggest you implement all methods as quickly as you can to gain growth for your Fiverr business from the beginning. All of these strategies are inexpensive or free. You just need to advertise your products to people you believe might be interested, and not to everybody.

Chapter 6: The System

There are just six short steps you must complete in order to earn some money from Fiverr as a part-time job.

A majority of these steps are very simple, so you must follow my directions and I'm sure you'll achieve results in a short time (Considering of the course you'll take actions!).

Step 1 - Set up Your Account

You must ensure you have your account correctly configured or else your customers will not believe in you and their money.

Step 2: Select the Selling Service

Once you've got your account setup then you'll need to pick one of the services you'll be able to provide. I'll help you choose the most effective and most profitable products to offer.

Step 3 - Design Your Own Gig

This is your sales letter.

In simple terms, if you're is a GIANT SUCK, then you WON"T receive any orders.

Step 4 - Add Your Extras

This is what makes the distinction between $300 monthly business and a $1,000 monthly one.

You must absolutely have EXTRA GOLD to give you to earn more money.

5. Beyond Fiverr

The fifth step is to think beyond Fiverr and think about other sites which offer similar services at more money.

Step 6 SEO Your Way to More Customers

The final step is to apply some SEO strategies to rank your web page's URL in Google as well as other search engines.

This will increase the number of customers you have.

Step 1 - Set up Your Account

There are 3 ways to sign-up on Fiverr. The first is to connect to your Facebook as well as Google+ to Fiverr and the final option is to create a free account.

I would recommend using the second option since you will be able to set up your profile more efficiently.

Visit http://fiverr.com and click on the button to begin selling.

Input the relevant information such as your email address, username and password.

IMPORTANT:

Pick a username closely related to your area of expertise. If you're not sure about your area of expertise, then you are able to revisit this portion later, after we've select our niche or market.

For further information, you must fill in as many details as you can to your account. Your potential customers will notice this, which is why you need to be professional, however, you must maintain the impression of being welcoming. Pick a profile picture that shows smiling. You can also include as an illustration of the work as your profile picture if work as an illustrator, or designer.

Step 2: Select the the Service to Sell
When choosing a service or niche I have just three needs.
1. I'm sure you'll be able to offer a high-quality service to this market (which means that you are aware of how to deliver this kind of service)
2. I'll deliver it to you quickly
3. A lot of people are purchasing it.
A.I is expected to provide quality services in this particular market (which means that you know how to provide this kind of service)

Write down your strengths and skills and select something you are able to excel at. Grab an eraser and a piece of paper.

B. I'm able to deliver it quickly

Users on Fiverr visit the site to do so for two reasons.

1. They'd like to have fast service
2. They'd like it to be cheap

Always deliver over and make sure you deliver it quickly

C. A lot of people have already bought it.

To determine if customers are already buying your new product or service. We then need to conduct an initial search on Fiverr.

Let's say that I'm proficient in writing articles as well as SEO backlinking. Let's find out if there's demand for it. When you type something in your search box, Fiverr will make a suggestion of possible keywords. These are the keywords you need to be aware of since people are looking for these terms.

It appears that there are a lot of companies selling this service, and that's an excellent sign. Do not be scared of competition. If your service is excellent, eventually clients will be drawn to you.

Remember that the beginning is always the most difficult part.

Another method of determining whether your product will be successful and not check for companies that offer an immediate turnaround of 24 hours.

If you can find services similar to this, then there are people who want prompt service.

The Creativity Niche

There are a myriad of services you can provide to your customers. You don't have to be limited by "what is popular" in the present. Sometimes, you must be innovative. Take a look at the most innovative ways that people make money with fiverr.

These services are fantastic in addition.

Check out this guy! (image below)
The reason you can't earn money from Fiverr is that you're lazy!
He has hundreds of positive reviews!
There are people who think this service is a joke, however the HELL is this man.
While this person is earning hundreds of dollars enjoying the work he is doing, many are working their 9-5 job with a sigh of discontent every minute of it.
If you're upset I'm sorry for that - my suggestion is to do something and test it. It's impossible to know whether it's going to generate income until you do

something about it and actually make an effort to market it.

Fiverr Tips To Start You On Your Way

To help you get started I've created the following list of possible jobs to earn money from.

These are only my personal favorite areas. You will definitely discover more lucrative niches as gain more experience.

The List

Product or Service Review

Amazon Product Review

SEO-related articles

SEO backlinks

Wordpress Installation

Web Design

Draw something

Copywriting

Blog post writing

Body Advertising

Book covers

Send an email
Make a postcard
Draw yourself
Videos Animations, Voice Overs

The easiest method is to locate a service that you can offer
This may sound simple, yet many people overlook it.
How do you locate an area of interest?
If you visit Fiverr's website, you'll be able to select categories from. From there, you can dig into the categories and select one.
Yep, that's it.
Begin with something you're exceptionally skilled at.

Step 3: Create Your Own Gig
If you're hoping to earn an enormous amount of money and gain hundreds

of clients, you must ensure that your business stands out.

Here's the guideline to follow to make an awesome gig that is a success.

Make sure to use high-quality images on your gigs

Take a look at this man's show

The picture is amazing I'm sure to make use of him the next time I require voice over.

The professional appearance suggests that his voice is worthy of hearing.

Make sure you use the Correct Keyword

Whatever it is you're offering be sure to make use of the keyword suggestions provided by Fiverr.

The Clear Title, the Description, and Category

Your title should correspond to the suggested keywords or whatever you're trying to promote.

Your category must also be in line with the service you provide.

Give a realistic delivery time

If you can deliver it within 24 hours, you should do it. But ensure that it's of good quality. If not, decide on a realistic for delivery of your services. You may also charge extra fees for customers who request their order to be prioritised.

Make clear the buyer's instructions

Take a look at the illustration below.

It's clear and easy to comprehend.

Here's a different example of a simple instruction

Step 4 - Add Your Extras

Here are some ways to earn more money with your services.

Create the service

There is no need to concentrate on a single niche, especially in times of tight money. Offer as many gigs as you can as you can. If you can attempt to use a an alternate username for each occasion.

Charge more for faster delivery

Ex.

Offer a better service

Ex.

Are you able to see the ways these services are linked?

Even if the customer pays $5 for the base service you may still provide additional services.

In the photo below, you'll be able to see that all of the services add up to a total value of

$155. Customers will not purchase the entire range of services However, if you only obtain 20% of this the total, you can raise your customer's value to about $30-35 per customer.

Each day, we will get 1 customer between $30 and $35, then we'll be able to reach our goal of $1,000/month.

35 * 30 = $1,050

Offer them more services and you'll increase the amount of money you earn each month.

Remember, you can only have 1 customer per day at $35/customer or It is possible to sell more, but you'll need to have 7 customers a day to get the $35 per day.

I'll pick the first at any time.

Additional examples of gigs from various areas.

- From the insanely amazing guy

From a press release service
- From a script writer

Step 5 Beyond Fiverr

The most effective way to earn money from Fiverr is to never use Fiverr for any reason.

This is what I mean If you have an existing business that is in place, along with your testimonials and reviews. You can then visit websites such as elance.com or upwork, and many other.

These people can charge more for the same services that you offer on Fiverr.

Why not make your own profile and search for those who are looking for your services.

Let's suppose you're offering book covers via Fiverr.

Go to elance.com and look up book covers.

People in this country pay much more. You can charge a higher rate on the platform than on fiverr. The only drawback is that you have to start over with no review of your profile on elance.

The great thing is that there are already testimonials and a work samples to show your customers. This shouldn't be a problem at all.J

Continue to repeat the procedure until you are able to increase your offerings.

There are many other websites similar to Fiverr You can also expand your services by advertising or creating your own profile on these sites:

Gigme5.com (jobs at $5)

Justafive.com (jobs at $5)

Tenrr.com (no charges, no jobs starting at $10)

Tenyt.com (jobs for just $10)

Fora20.com (jobs for only $20)

Gigbucks.com (jobs from $5 to $25)

Fittytown.com (jobs with a salary of $50)

Gigbay.com (jobs between $5 and $100)

Fiverrs.net (jobs with a starting price of $5)

Zeerk.com (jobs from $2-$100)

Tenbux.com (jobs for $5-10)

Uphype.com (jobs between $8 and $24)

Myntmarket.com (jobs from $8-$24)

Dollar3.com (jobs from $3 to $15)

Jobsfor10.com (jobs between $5 and $20)

Outsourcerr.com (jobs with a price of $5)

Gigrr.com (jobs between $5 and $100)

Cinkue.com (jobs for 5 euros)

Tennerrs.com (jobs for $10)

Ojl.net (jobs at $5)

Earner.net (jobs between $5 and $400)

Step 6 SEO Your Way to More Customers

Do you realize that you could earn more money making use of Fiverr to place your gigs on Google?

There are many people looking for services that aren't available on Fiverr If you are able to get your listing URL to rank on Google and Google, you will also attract these clients and earn more revenue!

It's really easy and straightforward to accomplish.

What I'd like for you to accomplish is employ at least five individuals using Fiverr (five five dollars worth of SEO services) and request them to create backlinks for your gig's url.

Here are some of the products you can purchase:

1 - Seo backlinks

2 - PBN backlinks

3. Social bookmarks

4. Article blasting

5. Social Backlinks

Pick five different services that have five-star ratings and make use of them.

All you need to do is give Google your URL and the keywords you would like to be ranked for on Google.

If I'm selling an ebook on Fiverr. I could provide the seller on Fiverr at least two keywords to choose from and the URL it will connect to.

URL: fiverr.com/myunqiuegigurl

Keywords:

Cover for ebook Fiverr

Cheap ebook cover

And you're done!

Send them the information and they'll take care of the rest for you.

Most people see results within thirty days, or even less.

Based on the level of competition, it could take as long as 3 months or longer if the keywords you are ranking for are highly sought-after or with a high volume.

Step by Step System Step by Step System

Follow these steps and you'll likely make some extra money online.

1. Find a service to offer

First, locate an online service that will sell the source I'm going to show you.

Please don't make this website available for sharing because only a handful of my business associates are aware of the site. Please keep this website to you.

2. Confirm the market

Next step would be to visit Fiverr and ensure there's an audience for the services. It's a simple research process and takes just some time to complete.

3. Create a Product Listing

This is the stage in which you'll make the gig list.

You need to ensure that you're writing something that convinces buyers to buy from you.

I'll provide you with the step-by-step procedure for how to accomplish it.

4. Sell More to Your Customers

Are you looking to earn the equivalent of $50 in a month? Then don't upsell your customers.

Do you want to earn 500 dollars per month? Make use of the EXTRA GIG feature in Fiverr and offer additional services.

5: How Do You Drive traffic to Your Listings

The final step is to redirect some customers to your site.

I'll teach you some strategies to drive customers to your website using Fiverr as well as other methods, too. It isn't enough to rely solely on Fiverr its own. It's a good idea If you adhere to some of the tips I'll provide throughout this book.

Are you ready?

Let's begin the course.

1 - Locate an item to sell

First, you must utilize SEO CLERK's service. SEO CLERK.

There are numerous $1 deals on this page that you can offer at $5 on Fiverr.

There are also offers between $5 and $20 which you can utilize as an upsell however we'll get into the upsell later.

To start, go to SEOCLERK.COM

Also, search for services that cost $1.

These are my top eight specific services I would recommend you market.

I'll give for you the fish!

To find the service you want Use the search button and then press enter.

Rearrange the services according to price. You'll be able to find the lowest priced services first.

They are the ones that I would recommend that you resell at $5-$50 on Fiverr.

TOP 8 SERVICES to SELL

A . - Facebook LIKES

Facebook remains the biggest the most popular social media and it won't alter until 18-36 months from today.

It's an excellent market according to me.

This is the perfect opportunity for newbies because there's a market waiting to be discovered.

B. Followers of Twitter

There are many people who need to boost their social media followers. They can use social evidence.

This service is not going to end anytime very soon.

This $1 service could be easily sold at 10 times the original price.

C. - Followers on Instagram

Don't be fooled, Instagram is expanding.

I think it's at an infancy stage, but will continue to expand, particularly for those between 20 and 35 years old.

D - Snapchat Services
Snapchat is exploding at the moment. There's no better time to join than now.
Snapchat services are priced higher right now but you are able to sell it at a higher price.

E SEO articles SEO articles
This service will not ever cease to exist.
Information articles are essential and will be required for the rest of time.
Every article you read online is an article in various types.
The main difference between SEO articles and normal content is that SEO ARTICLES are specifically created

for the purpose of optimizing search engines as well as some terms were included in order to attract SEO lovin.

The F-SEO Backlink

SEO BACKLINKS are used to help a website rank higher in Google.

So long as SEO exists, then this service will remain sought-after.

G. Article Submission

This is a method of posting backlinks.

It's different from the usual SEO backlinks.

It is also profitable, due to exactly the same reasons like the previous service.

As long as Google exists, then users will continue to purchase the service.

H - YouTube Views & Comments

Youtube is the most trusted source in the field of videos and this will not change in the next five years.

Sell your services that are related to Youtube and get a guaranteed portion from the industry.

2. Confirm the market

This is the easiest process since you'll have to visit Fiverr and look up the service you'd like to offer.

If you can find people who have many reviews and sales, then it's a great market to choose to target.

Simply type in your service's name, and then take a look at the reviews and ratings for your service.

Are there any other people selling the same product you are trying to sell?

Good!

Then there's an actual market!

FACEBOOK LIKES

Twitter Followers

Followers on Intagram

This model has a smaller market share based on the reviews, however I'm sure it'll be profitable.

After you have confirmed your market size The following step would be to make an online listing.

First You must make your own profile and account first.

Make sure you complete the profile completely and make sure that you don't leave anything out.

3 - Create a product Listing

I'm going to teach this chapter step-by-step with an examples.

Let's say that you wish to offer an GEO Filter for the SNAPCHAT.

(Here's the show we'll take as a model)

https://www.fiverr.com/owldesignlab /make-snapchat-geofilter-for-anywhere-in-the-world?context=advanced_search&con

text_type=rating&context_referrer=se
arch_gigs&pos=1&funnel=a3775077-
5e09-4363-9c48-d5d464fce8f4

1. TITLE

It is the first thing to do. explain what you have to offer or offer to sell.

Example:

Ich will... create Snapchat GeoFilter for your local company.

I'll... develop an SNAPCHAT filter within three days, or less.

2 - IMAGES/VIDEO

Next step would be to create a an attractive image that is relevant with your services.

Be sure to mention the average delivery time and the number of revisions You are allowed.

3 3 DESCRIPTION

Next step to provide your information! Simply call the market you want to target and explain what you're selling them.

4. PORFOLIO or SAMPLE

Give them the hyperlink on your website to show off the portfolio.

You may utilize the portfolio of the seller originally, however, you must seek his permission prior to doing so.

You can also upload your portfolio into the section titled IMAGES.

5. Give them choices.

Give them the package and the items that are included. The package.

Also, don't forget note down important information or directions for ordering.

Make sure you request any information you require from them.

You do not want to create confusion regarding providing the service.

6 How to order

The final step is to provide them with instructions regarding how to place an order and the steps to expect after they make their purchase.

How can they place an place an order? When are you due to deliver?

Are there any changes?

How can they contact you?

This can help customers to make orders, thus increasing your profits.

That's it!

This is the easy 6 steps of writing your gig list.

Of course, there's GIG EXTRAS, so we'll talk about it in the following chapter.

4. Increase the value of your customers

I have a single procedure to create GIG EXTRAS.

Just copy and paste the entire thing.

It isn't a good idea in any way, but If it's working and it's working, why should you alter it?

It's unlikely that you're looking for this kind of solution and I apologise however it is logical to simply copy the method that is working already.

If you decide to create your extra jobs, take a look at your competition and take a look at what they're doing.

You also need to confirm and make sure that your seller is able to provide the service at the rates you are setting.

It is recommended that you purchase the service at a less expensive price to still earn money from it.

You may offer different variations of your services, however generally speaking the more expensive the quicker delivery time should be, and the additional options.

Features like:

1. Original file will be provided to the buyer.

/Providing source files

2 - Different colors

3. More revisions

4 - Faster delivery

5 - Add additional illustrations (for banners, images) and add additional

words (articles) Add additional hyperlinks (backlinking services)

Here are some great examples of extra gigs that you can duplicate.

Snaphat Geofilter

Facebook Likes

Social marketing in general

HOW DO I MARKET THE UPSELL

Here's a four-step guide for upselling your customers.

The next one will be concise and straight short and to the point. Simply follow the instructions and let the outcome speak for themselves.

Step 1. Initial Contact Following They Purchased

Do this the day following the time you delivered the service.

Ask them to leave you their feedback and offer them a reward for buying your first service.

Step 2 - The First Upsell

After three days, you can ask whether they require another service.

It is important to share with them the URL to the GIG EXTRAS.

Tell them that you'll give them a discount, or quicker delivery if they can place an order within 24 hours.

Step 3. Second Upsell

If they didn't purchase the extra gigs, it's okay.

You can contact them again in a couple of several weeks.

Be sure to give them an exclusive item or privilege to customers who place an order through you CUSTOM ORDER.

4. Last Chance

If they haven't yet bought the item, wait one month before calling them once more.

In this case you must give them a the free sample or any extra value before you make any sales.

The value that you give upfront could be purchased for $5, however you'll get it gratis.

You can then ask them to purchase your extra GIFTS (which you'll create as custom GIGS).

Make sure you'll still earn profits. The cost of an upsell should be at minimum 4 times the original price of your service provider.

5: How Do You Drive traffic to Your Listings

Next step getting people to view your product listings.

Here are the best methods to drive the most traffic to your business.

Fiverr is itself

One of the most effective methods to gain immediate attention for your service is optimizing the contents of your Fiverr listing.

Be sure to do these things to have a greater chance of appearing first on the page each when someone type your key keywords or keywords.

1. Put the keyword in the title

2. Put the keyword in the tags

3 - use your keyword as the title of your video

4. In your description, ensure that you use keywords that relate to your main keywords. For instance, if your job is focused around twitter, figure out ways to include twitter in your description.

Twitter, followers, followers favorite, tweets, followers, and others details on your description.

5 - Invite your family and friends to come to your website

Like always...

Begin your keyword research using the search bar method that I have already explained to you.

Another thing you can do is visit Google keyword planner , and then search for the service you want to advertise.

Say you chose, article spinning.

Find it by searching for it, and then find the keywords related to it which you can use as well.

Join niche forums

Whatever your market is, try to join a forum related to it and add your service on the signature part of your profile. Every time you make a post, members see your service below that post. A warning though, never ever spam the heck out of people's conversations. Make sure that you actually say and give something of value. Don't be the guy who's just there to sell something. Be a valuable part of the community. I swear, it's gonna be worth your time and effort.

Facebook

Join pages related to your service. Provide real, actionable value and then add them as friends. Once they started to like you and once you start providing great value to the community, you can ask them to buy your service.

Comments on blogs

As always, provide something worth reading and then promote your service.

Youtube

This is my favorite method.

You just have to make a bunch of 30 second videos (try to be creative and funny if you can) promoting your products on Fiverr. Always put your link below the videos. Another benefit of doing this is you'll get some SEO love from Youtube (because you put your url in your youtube description).

When you create your video, simply follow this formula:

1 - Introduce yourself

2 - Tell them what you're selling

3 - Give them the benefits of what you're selling

4 - Ask to click the link below

5rrsuccessforum.com

Promote your services in this website. To stand out on this website, you must have an amazing or unique video promoting your service. You don't even have to do the video yourself, hire someone on Fiverr to shoot a video for you. I recommend that you hire a sexy young lady or some good looking guy to promote your product. It'll sky rocket your conversion. Guaranteed.

Current customers

Once you start doing some of my suggestions, you'll get your first few customers. Take care of them and treat them with respect. Give more than they expected if you must. If you can get repeat customers, then their yours forever. Repeat customers are hands down the best customers in the planet.

Chapter 7: Choose A Service

One of the keys to having a successful Fiverr based freelancing business is by doing something you enjoy doing.

You don't necessarily have to love it, but doing something you enjoy doing is key to making work fun for you.

If you dread every second of working on a specific project, then the final result won't be satisfactory to you and your client.

What I'm going to give you in this chapter are the most profitable categories to target this year (and I believe that they will continue to grow more in the following years).

So we want something that can make money now, but at the same time, will make even more money in the future.

We want an established kind of service that will be profitable in the long game.

THE TOP 10 LIST

I have a list of the top 10 services that you may want to offer yourself on Fiverr.

My list is not based on data or any study done by outside party.

This is just based on my 9 years of experience with Internet Marketing in general.

So follow my advice with a grain of salt.

What I can promise you is that I didn't just pull this list out of my butt.

I know some people who are making good money offering these types of services.

So here they are and why you should consider offering one of them.

#1 – WordPress Services

If you're interested with the tech stuff part of a running a website, then this is for you.

What I like about this category is it's so big that you can pretty much become "just" a WordPress guy. You don't need any other skills or services to really make a killing.

Being a WordPress expert is enough.

Why? Because there's lots of different "mini services" that you can offer related to WP.

If you look at WordPress on Fiverr, you can see different types of subcategories like...

If you're into tech stuff, then this should definitely be at the top of your list.

#2 – Book Covers

The rise of self-publishing has given many freelancers that opportunity of a lifetime.

Today, thousands of people are joining the self-publishing game.

And guess what type of service every single book needs?

Yup, book covers.

For book covers, you can choose to focus on either fiction or non-fiction.

You can even specialize on a certain genre in the future.

#3 – Proofreading & Editing

Another service that benefits from the rise of
self-publishing is Proofreading & Editing.

Although not all self-publishers use a proofreader or editor, a lot of them are still flocking Fiverr (and other websites) looking for a proofreader to make their books better.
If you love reading books and if you're a "the devil is in the detail" kind of person, then this service is for you.

#4 – T-Shirt Designs

In the past 4 years, I've seen so many online courses got launched in this industry.

People love personalize t-shirts and a lot of marketers are making money off of it.

If you can design a great t-shirt, then you can make lots of money online.

Even if you're not a skilled designer yet, you should still consider this category (I'll teach you how to get better fast on the next chapter).

#5 – YouTube SEO

Here's a fact.
Almost everyone you know regularly watch videos on YouTube.

Heck, I think my mom watches more videos on YouTube more than I do (she loves those cooking recipe channels).

The point is, a lot of people are publishing their videos and a lot of them wants to get seen.

And one of the best ways to get seen on YouTube is to rank your video on the first page of the search engines (YouTube and Google).

Offering this type of service could be a really profitable one for you. YouTube isn't going anywhere. It's here to stay.

#6 – PBN Backlinks Creation

Another SEO related service is backlinking.

Basically, it's about putting inbound or outbound links from one website to another.

And the best type of backlink to use right now is the one called Private Blog Networks.

To offer this service, you can either create your own set of backlinks (around $50 each minimum) or you can just buy a PBN that's already an authority website that can be used for your service.

On average, 1 good PBN link (Page Rank - PR 5-6) can be sold for around $20. PR 7-9 can be sold for around $200 each.

#7 – Articles & Blogposts

Even though blogging hasn't been as hot as before, people still need content.

This is where you come in.
You can write articles or high quality blogposts for other bloggers or content creators.

This is one of the easiest way to enter the freelancing industry.

A warning though, try not to get stuck in the "cheap phase".

This is where you only charged $5 per 500-word article.

Get your experience and then start charging more by offering your services with premium prices ($30-$100 per article).

#8 – Podcast Related Services

I love this one.

It's like WordPress in a way that there's a lot of mini services that you can offer your potential customers.
You can offer to create the introduction, some voiceover, transcription, music creation, audio editing, etc.

This is a medium that I can confidently recommend that you focus on. It's the new radio and just like YouTube, it's not going anywhere anytime soon.

#9 – Social Content

Social contents can be a YouTube video, a tutorial, a 300 word Facebook Post, an Infographic, etc.

Anything that be used as content for Facebook, Twitter, YouTube,

Instagram and other social media entities.

#10 – E-commerce Store (Store Creation, Store Optimization)

Another business model that really had a boom the past 5 years is ecommerce.

There are tons of new people creating their ecommerce website. And most of them are clueless on how to do it.

You can offer service like website creation (via Shopify or other platforms) and website optimization (editing the website, making it more user friendly, optimizing the add to cart buttons, etc.).

Another thing that you can do is to learn to drive traffic to these ecommerce websites.

New marketers are desperate for traffic.

They want to make a sale and you can help them do it.

You can offer to manage their Facebook Ads or their Google Adwords. Creating their website may earn you $30-$100, but managing their ad accounts can make you thousands.

LAST WORD ON CHOOSING A SERVICE
When you're choosing a service, don't think of it as the end all be all of the entire process.

Think of that service as the entry for more expensive services that you can offer in the future.

Sure, you can make $1,000-$3,000+ on Fiverr, but the real money comes when you start leveraging your current skills and offering them at premium prices.

Now, let's talk about how you can get good fast in your chosen skill.

Get Good at It

The next step is to actually get good at the service you want to offer.

And NO, you cannot "fake it till you make it" your way to expertise.

The good news is you don't have to be the best when it comes to the service you are selling.

You just have to be good enough.

Remember, you are selling on Fiverr.

Most services will be at the $5-$50 price range.

So good enough is actually good enough in this case.

Most of the services I mentioned in chapter 1 can be learned in 2-4 weeks. Here are the things you can do to get good really fast.

#1 – Practice Marathon

The best way to get good at a specific skill is to practice it over and over again.

What I recommend is that you schedule a practice session for the next 2-4 weeks.

2 hours per day at the minimum.

That's the allotted that I'm going to ask you to invest in yourself.

You'll be amaze at how good you'll become just by practicing something 2 hours per day every day for the next 30 days.

Seriously, you'll be at the top 10% immediately and you can now offer that service confidently.

#2 – Do It for Free

If you want to really forced yourself to get good, then offer your service for FREE.

Find some Facebook groups who might need your service.

This is also a really good way to get some testimonials for your service.

You don't need to do this for the next 30 days.

Just one or two free projects is enough.

#3 – Apprentice

This is the original way of learning.

Someone spends time with a mentor until he becomes worthy of offering the same kind of service to other people.

Find someone who is already an expert and ask to work for him for free.

Spending some time with an expert is a priceless strategy to get good really fast. You'll know the shortcuts, the techniques and secrets you'll never get elsewhere.

If an opportunity like this comes up, grab it and maximize that experience.

#4 - Books & Online Courses

Not all of us can find a mentor.

This is a cheap and fast way to learn more about your service.

I recommend that you take courses from Udemy, Skillshare and CreativeLive.

Most of the courses are at the $10-$100 price range.

Imagine learning to create a WordPress website for $10.

Once you got that skill, nobody can ever take that away from you.

You can now offer that skill for $10 or more over and over again.

#5 – Hire a Coach

Look, if someone isn't willing to hire you as an apprentice, then you gotta pay your way to get that experience.

You don't need to hire a very expensive coach.

Find someone who isn't currently teaching that skill. Find someone who is an expert but doesn't have any info marketing products.

Then offer to have lunch or coffee with him. Then you can ask if he can mentor you for a fee.

It's a win-win situation.

He gets paid for his knowledge and you get good really fast by learning how to provide a great service to your customers.

Once you're good enough to offer a service, it's time to create your Fiverr account.
Set Up Your Account the Right Way

This is a chapter that most people can skip if they want to. So go to chapter 4 now if you already have a complete basic profile information.

Creating an account is simple and pretty much dumb-proof.

However, I do want to remind you of some of the things that you can do to make your profile more enticing to your potential clients.

To register, go to Fiverr.com and click Become a Seller.

Then go to your profile and change your profile picture.

Then upload a close up picture of you smiling.

I have no idea why but this seem to get the attention of most buyers.

Then on the description, put 1-2 sentence describing what you offer.

The language will be English by default.

If you know any other language, then make sure that you put it in the Languages section.

Then put your skills on the SKILLS section.

Then for education, put your degree (if any) because some people do consider it even though it really has nothing to do with the service you are offering.

Save all of these and you're finished.

Now it's time to sell our service. It's time to create a product listing.
Product Listing That Works

There different ways to create a listing description and there's no one superior way to do it.

Different tactics works for different markets.

This is my way of doing it and it works well for me.

For beginners, you can choose to follow this and then put your own touch later.

To create a gig, just go to SELLING and then click Gigs.

Next, click Create a New Gig.

For your title, I want you to create something straight forward and bounded by time.

E.g.

I will give you 3,000 YouTube views in 3 days.

I will fix your WordPress bug in 12 hours.

Next, choose the right category for your service.

Then in the tags, put keywords that people may use to search for your service.

You can find these keywords by looking at your competitor's listing.

It's in the bottom of their listing below the reviews.

For the pricing, I always create 3 different packages.

My service could offer more quantity or faster timeframe for completion, or both.

Here's an example:

In this case, I offer quantity in a different way. I offer front cover, back cover and both of them combined, plus 3d.
If you're selling YouTube Views, then you can offer something like this:

A – 1,000 Views in 24 hours

B – 2,000 Views in 24 hours

C – 3,000 Views in 24 hours

For the actual price, I usually start with $10, then $15 and then $20.

It could be different for you.

Look at the market and the competition and see what others are doing.

Personally, I prefer to be the expensive one in the market.
So if everybody is selling at $10, I will start with $15 or $20.

Next, you can offer Extra Gigs by adding faster time of completion, revisions and source files.

In this case, I added faster delivery and then the source files for an additional $5-$10.

ALWAYS, ALWAYS, ALWAYS put these extra gigs.

These are almost free money. You don't really need to do much more to offer a source file for example.

So whatever other offer you can add, don't hesitate to add it there as part of the Extra Gigs.

Next is the Description.

The description is tricky to teach since there's no one way that works for all markets.

But I think that this simple way that I'm gonna teach you will work for you.

Here's an example:

#1 – Pre-Title

First, mention the service. What is it? Basically, whatever it is you are offering...

#2 – What You Do

Next, mention what you are offering. This time, you'll add more details.

You can even be more specific here.

You can say...

Hi, I do Non-Fiction Business Book covers with fast turnaround time.
#3 – What You'll Get

Then you'll mention what they will get as part of the package.

#4 – What I Need

Then you'll just mention the info you need in order to successfully provide the service.

#5 – Call to Action

Lastly, ask them to buy the service.

And that's it. My motto has always been simple is better.

And in this case, it is really true and it works!

For the Requirements, you'll just ask the buyer for all the details you need in order to fulfill the service.

E.g.

GALLERY

This is one of the most important part of your listing.

The goal of your gallery is to grab their attention so they will click your listing.

Another one is to show some examples of your work if possible (not all services can be shown through pictures).

I cannot teach you how to edit a Gallery image but I can show you some examples of gallery that works and some that just plain sucks.

AWESOME

NAHHHH

(witty but it won't sell)

(this is good enough, but it won't sell as much)

Once you uploaded your main image + some examples of your work, just click continue and then hit Publish Gig.

It'll be LIVE in a few minutes and it's now ready to get some orders.

Upselling Customers for 2x More Profits

The different between the $500 per month and the $2k-$3k Fiverr freelancer is not the skills or the quality of work or even the categories.

The real difference is in the upsell.

A lot of people will be too lazy to do this.

That's the reason they will only earn a few hundred bucks of extra income per month.

If you want to earn full-time income, then you gotta put in full-time work.

That doesn't mean you have to work 5x harder and longer.

Nope, that means spending a little bit more time upselling customers to your additional or other related services.

So how do you do up-sells?

Well Fiverr allows you to message people through Fiverr itself.

What I do is I send a series of messages from Day 1 to Day 30.

After that, I usually just stop messaging them or get back to them again after 3-4 months.

Every customer that you get can have a higher value in terms of money as soon as you learned how to upsell.

Fortunately, it's simple and very easy to do.

I normally send at least 5 messages in a span of 30 days offering them some additional services.

THE SCHEDULE

The messages will be send at this time frame.

Day 1 (from the day you deliver the final service that he first bought) – The Thank You

The first message I send is always a thank you message.

They just bought from you and you need to thank them for their patronage.
E.g.

Hey Arry,

Thanks again for getting my X Service and I hope that you're happy with what you get.
If you need anything else, please don't hesitate to contact me here on Fiverr.

Also, I do have some other services related to what you got today. You can check them out here:

www.fiverrlink.com

Thanks again and have a good day!

Talk Soon,

Your Name

Day 3 – The Offer

The next step is to offer them some kind of discount for your current services.

E.g.

Hi Arry,

I'm running a discount promo for my loyal customers until XX day (day 7). If you're interested in getting a 30% discount for X service, kindly reply to this message and maybe we could work something out.

This offer will only last till X date (day 7) and I wouldn't want you to miss it since I really had a good time working with you.

Talk Soon,

Your Name

Day 7 – Last Chance

On day 7, you'll just mention that the offer for a 30% discount is expiring today.

E.g.
Hi Arry,

Remember that 30% discount for any of my service that I offered you a few days ago?

Well, the offer end TODAY.

If you want to take advantage of this offer, just let me know by replying back to this message.

After 12 midnight today, I'll close the offer and I'll be focusing more on providing the services bought by my clients.

Check out this link to find out more about this offer.

www.fiverrlink.com

Talk Soon,

Your Name
Day 14 – Personalize Offer

In this part, you'll just mention that you can also do personalize services made just for their needs.

E.g.

Hi Arry,

You probably don't know this but I also do personalize services, tailor made just for your needs.

So if you need anything done related to Podcasting (or whatever your service is), just let me know and I'll be here happy to help you.

Alright, have a good day.

Talk Soon,

Your Name
Day 30 – Do You Still Need Me?

This is the part where you just ask them if they need anything from you.

At this point, you're just trying to know if they're still interested. It's like the last hurrah to know if they will buy or not.

Example message:

Hey Arry,

I haven't heard from you in a while.

I hope you're doing well.

30 days ago, you bought X service from me and I would like you to know that I really appreciate your business.

If you need anything else, just let me know and I'll reply back as soon as I can.

Here are some services that I currently offer:

fiverrService1link.com
fiverrService2link.com

fiverrService2link.com

Talk Soon,

Your Name

- - -

Upselling is an important part of your business.

Not all customers will buy again, but remember this.

It 5x easier to sell to current customers than to sell to new customers.

So follow this upsell method.

Just keep at it and you'll eventually get YES'ES.

This is where the real money is made.

Learn to do it and you'll prosper.

Chapter 8: Choose A Service

There's a lot of ways to choose a service to sell.

The service that you will choose should be something that you're interested in (even just a little bit), something that you're willing to learn in and it must be something that people are already buying.

WAYS TO CHOOSE A SERVICE

1 – Start With What You Know

Always start with what you know.
What are your current skills? What are
your experiences?

What I want you to do is grab a piece
of paper and write all of the jobs or
any professional experience you had.

You'll be surprise about some
forgotten skill or experience you had
that you actually love to do.
You should also start with what you
know because there are times where
you could get burned out. The love for
what you are doing and the skill level
that you have will get you through
that phase.

If you hate what you're doing, then there's no way that you can make a long-term business out of that skill.

Combine these two when searching for a service to sell.

Interest & Skill.

Are you skilled enough to sell a service on that category?

Are you and interested enough to learn and get better?

2 – Top Fiverr Sub-Categories

The next method is to focus on already profitable categories on Fiverr.

What are these categories?

To be honest, I don't have hard-proof data to prove this, so I'm just gonna rely on my own experience.

IMO, the best categories are the following:

(Note: you can see all of these on Fiverr's home page)

GRAPHICS & DESIGN

A – Book Covers and Packaging

B – Web & Mobile Design

C – T-Shirt Design

D – Infographics

DIGITAL MARKETING

A – SEO

B - Content Marketing

C – Video Marketing

D – Ecommerce Marketing

WRITING & TRANSLATION

A – Resumes & Cover Letters

B – Proofreading & Editing

C – Articles & Blogposts

VIDEO & ANIMATION

A – Whiteboard & Explainer Videos
B – Intros

C – Editing & Post Production

MUSIC & AUDIO

A – Voiceover

PROGRAMMING & TECH

A – WordPress

B- Website Builders

C- Ecommerce

BUSINESS

A – Virtual Assistant

B – Presentations
As you can see, there's a lot of possible sub-categories to target. Try to choose from the ones that I mention above.

These are proven sub-categories with lots of active buyers in it.

3 – Top Freelancing Categories

A best-selling category on Fiverr may not necessarily be a best-selling category on other freelancing websites.

So make sure that you also search for other services that may be profitable on Fiverr even though it's not on the sub-categories that I mention earlier.

According to Matt Barrie (in his interview with James Altucher), the best services to start as a brand new freelancer are the following:

A – Software Architecture

B – Web Testing & Scraping

C - Web Design & Development

D – Graphic Design & Photoshop

E – Illustration

F – 3D Rendering

G – Writing

H – Video Animation

I – App Development

Although these are much harder skills to learn, they can also be better for long term profitability.

Source:

http://thecusp.com.au/this-infographic-shows-how-you-can-make-2000-in-a-weekend/14574

Now that you already chose your service (you did it, right?). You can now start learning more about it so you can become a legit expert on that topic.

Become an Expert

What's an expert anyway?

Is it someone who has 20 years of experience and 3,000 projects in his portfolio?

Or is it someone who can do the work better than most people do?

I believe in the latter description of what an expert is.

So there you have it, you don't necessarily have to have years of experience to start selling your services on Fiverr.

You just need to be a little bit better on the job compared to most people.

Thing is, you can actually be better than most people just by doing the things that I'm gonna suggest you do.

Heck, give yourself 4 weeks of practice and you'll be better than 50% of the population in whatever skill you choose.

Why?

Because people are lazy.

On one hand, I've been creating book covers for 2 years now and I never really got to improved my skill.

Why?

Because I'm too lazy to go beyond my current skills and I'm too lazy to learn more about it.

So don't be like me!

On the other hand, I've been learning to run Facebook ads and I've gotten better at it in the past 2 years.

Why?
Because I'm constantly learning, taking courses and reading books. I'm taking action and I'm evaluating my results.

The most important thing to remember is to have focus and deliberate constant action.

THINGS TO DO TO BECOME AN EXPERT

1 – Read Books

Most of the skills that you can sell on Fiverr can be learn for $20 from a book.

Want to learn how to code?

Go read a book.

Want to learn how to edit WordPress websites?

Buy a manual, read it.
2 - Take Online Courses

If you're not a reader, then you can also take online courses.

Personally, I prefer this method because I'm a visual kind of person.

I like learning by seeing how it's done.

You should seriously consider taking online courses.

They're cheap as heck nowadays and you can start seeing progress just by following what the instructor said in his videos. I know! Too simple right? Go figure!

3 – Work for Free

Another method that you can do to get practice and experience is to work for free.

I know what you're thinking.

No, you're not gonna work for free and devaluate your worth.

Well, stop being an egotistic as&hole and start doing anything that may get you closer to your goals.

4 – Ask Someone to Mentor You

This is one of the best ways to become an expert fast.

Ask someone to personally teach you how to do a specific skill.

I recommend that you learn the basics yourself and then hire someone to mentor you personally when it comes to the advance stuff.

Trust me, the $ you'll spent will be worth it.

5 – Practice Consistently

The most important task of them all.

Practice every day. Practice consistently.

I suggest that you practice your skills at least 2 hours per day on weekdays and at least 1 hour per day on weekends.

You'll be surprise at how good you'll become in 4-8 weeks of doing deliberate practices.

And don't just practice for the sake of practice.

Aim for improvement. Do somethings that you won't normally do. Aim to get better and be honest with yourself.

Are you doing great work or are you doing mediocre work?

Yes or No?

Yes?

Then go on and continue that work

No?

Then work hard even more!

CONSISTENCY.

That's the keyword to your success.

SIGN UP ON FIVERR

Before you create your listing, please sign up for a free account here:

https://www.fiverr.com/join

Make sure that you compete all the required information.

Create a Fiverr Listing

Your listing will serve as your salesman in print.

Luckily for us, it's not that complicated to create one.

Just go to your dashboard and click GIGS.

Then add add a new gig.

TITLE

Mention your service and the time frame in your title.

Keep it simple and short.

The purchaser must know precisely what you're selling through the title of the product.

CATEGORY

Fiverr can automatically recommend the correct category based on your name.

You could also copy your rivals should you choose to.

TAGS

Copy the strategies your competitors are using.

Your keywords are the tags. These are the words people are looking for when searching for services similar to yours.

There are competitors' names below the reviews in their listings.

PACKAGINGS

Always provide 2 or 3 different options for your services.

Packages can easily boost the amount you earn by 2x.

I would recommend to give birth within three days.

Then, you can offer unlimited revisions.

Choose the file you'll submit after the project is completed.

For covers for books or graphic layouts, I would suggest you offer only JPG and then provide the different file types (source files) in addition to gigs in exchange for more money.

The majority of people prefer to start with just $5.

If you don't have clients or prior experience and you're not sure if you're qualified, then it's time to.

After reading some reviews I would recommend using the 10, 15, 20, price.

EXTRA GIFTS

Add quick delivery as well as other services as part of your additional gig.

DESCRIPTION

Here's the secret to writing great descriptions.

Copy your competitor's offer and modify the language based on the offer.

Wait , what?

Do you think this advice is real?

Yes it is.

Let's suppose you're selling ebook covers.

Look at the top-selling products in that area and include some more words to your proposal.

This man is a savior with nearly 300 reviews.

What I'm going to do is revise this proposal and modify it to my liking.

Example:

The best eBook Cover Designer in town!

Hello, I design eBook covers in a fast turnaround times.

- Effective Communication

- 100% Money Back Guarantee

Unlimited Revisions

(Please Check My Portfolio Below)

What you'll get

Front Cover

Back Cover

3D Cover

Unlimited Revisions, 100 100% Money Return Refunds are unlimited and 100% Money Back

What I Need:
Here are some links to help you decide on the book layout you'd like including title, sub-titles and the category of your book

Click the arrow and CLICK to order now.

There's no single method for writing descriptions.

Simply copy and change the text and then test it to see to see if it is working for you. Most likely it will, particularly in the case that you received this description from someone who is selling many items on Fiverr.

FAQ

For the FAQ, write questions and answers they might want to ask.

Don't fill in this section in case you don't have client or experience yet.

You can also duplicate the strategies of your competitors and put it in the same Q and A. Simply do the same thing with the title and modify it slightly.

REQUIREMENTS

Make the rules obligatory.

These are the details you require from the client to complete the transaction.
GALLERY
For gig pictures I suggest you include a single image that will promote your service. You can also include illustrations of your work on the following ones, If you can.

Thus, 1 art work and 4 portfolios are enough.

(artwork)

(portfolios)

Upload your photos and click VERIFY TODAY for your account to be published.

The Best 12 Fiverr Methods

What distinguishes the five/six and four figure earners is the way they conduct themselves and beliefs they adhere to.

These are the important things you must keep in mind if you are looking to become a reputable and successful Fiverr freelancer.

1. They ask for feedback

Always, ALWAYS, ALWAYS seek feedback.

It doesn't matter whether you have either a negative or positive response. The most important thing is that you can learn from the experience, so that you can become better at your art.

After each service you perform, you should contact your client within a few days to ask questions what quality of service you provided. Was he pleased? Do you think he would order from us again? recommend someone else who needs the same services?

2. Refund with questions Answered

Always offer a refund to your customer regardless of the reason.

It's true that this may sound inconvenient to your. However, trust me when I say that you'll be more relaxed and less stressed if you're not thinking about a single problem in the butt.

Always ask for the reason. You can refund the amount even if he decided not to provide the reason, but always request one.

The feedback you'll get from the refund is priceless.

If you do this you will avoid making the same mistake , and get lower refunds in the future.

3. Delivery in the earliest possible time Be sure to deliver by the deadline or earlier, if it is possible.

Customers are thrilled when they're hoping to receive something on the 18th, only to receive it in the 16th.

Try this.

Give something that has the delivery date of four days, and deliver it on the second day at no additional cost.

Your customers will be thrilled with you!

Of course, you can find additional gigs that offer speedier delivery at a cost However, you must take a look.

4 - Provide More than What is asked for

Over-promise and over-deliver.

Nothing in the world of marketing will ever be able to match the quality of service you offer your clients.

Concentrate on doing amazing work and always deliver more than you have promised.

5 - Sell the Customers on Upsells

Some of your customers will be willing to buy from you. This is why you must keep them in contact and ask them if they require any other items.

Personally, I prefer to communicate with the people I love at least once per every week during the following four weeks, then every 3 months following that.

Give them a incentive to continue buying from you.

Inform them about the latest offers as well as your special offers.

6 - Reply Rapidly

Sometimes, it's not an issue of the work's quality.

Sometimes, it's about responding quickly to their messages or questions.

Try to respond promptly and don't keep them waiting more than 12 days for an response.

7 - Honesty

You must be honest and transparent with your customers. Be honest with your.

If you aren't able to finish the task in 12 hours, do not promise to finish it in 12 hours.

Simply be transparent as well as let people know you're working hard to provide high-quality services.

8 - They concentrate on a single or two categories

Don't be entangled by opportunities that are available now.

Concentrate on a couple of areas and become really skilled in that particular area.

If you attempt to be an expert in more than two categories in a row, you'll end up in the middle and will be burned out at the final.

9 - They're Not Getting Their Hands Full

Don't take every client you meet.

If you're certain that you'll be fully booked for the next two weeks, don't think about selling a new service for the sake of earning an additional $30.

It's better to let go of this $30 than lose potential long-term clients due to the fact that your current work-product is shoddy.

10 They Love Their Work

There will be times when you'll get angry and exhausted.

Your passion for what you do can help you get through that stage.

11 - They Practice Consistently to Improve

I've mentioned it before, but I'm going to bring it up once more.

It is essential to practice regularly to improve your art.

Keep in mind that there are other people similar to you, looking to earn money online while working at the comfort of their homes.

12 . They Take Initiative

If you find something that isn't right with the project , or something unclear about it Do not be afraid to ask the client.

You can ask questions, but not to the extent that you're already irritating the customer every two hours.

Be proactive.

Determine the problem and come up with the solution that works most efficiently with the time of time you have.

Chapter 9: The Cherry On Top

In closing, I'd like to share with you the additional bits and pieces that can aid in providing an excellent experience as well as more potential income. You've completed the majority of the work and the advertising is done; all you have to do is add few additional details that you can add to the end of your profile as well as your gig on Fiverr.

Other items to include

People will be looking at your profile and your work and look for trustworthy information and solid experience in the industry in which you're promoting your services.
I would suggest adding all qualifications you've earned in the

section on education on your account. Check all of you social accounts Fiverr is not a fan of working with customers outside the platform. This is merely to provide professional proofand not to post them on your profiles. Be sure to highlight your distinctions, outstanding professional work and highly prestigious collaborations.

The more details you include to your profile and on gigs the more potential customers will be enticed to purchase from you.

How to become an Fiverr affiliate

The last thing I'd like to add to help you earn more money through Fiverr is to become an affiliate. This means that you promote Fiverr on other platforms than the Fiverr website (on your blog or YouTube channel, podcast, Facebook, Instagram, and so on.). If someone purchases by clicking your hyperlink, you earn an amount of the sale (usually generously).

This could range between 10 and 45 dollars for the first purchase made by a new customer, and the cost of a

The percentage you earn is based on the type of affiliate program you choose.

It is possible to earn more income as an affiliate selling by advertising Fiverr on various platforms like websites and blogs, YouTube, Facebook, Instagram, Pinterest, LinkedIn podcasts, emails - and the list continues.

As an Fiverr Affiliate, you will receive personalized shared links. It is just a matter of placing them in a wise manner online and then refer visitors to any Fiverr site which is the most appropriate for your customers. Customers who click your links and sign-up are automatically assigned the account you have created!

Be aware that as an affiliate of Fiverr associate, you will have the chance to promote the following Fiverr products, including Fiverr.com, Fiverr Learn, and AND.CO. Each link will take users to the appropriate Fiverr product and allow you to be entitled to the correct commission.

Conclusion

Thanks for taking the time to read this book.

At this point, you should be able to see how everything works.

I hope you act and follow the guidelines I provided in this book.

If you don't act, you've just wasted a few seconds (or many hours) of your time reading this book.

This book isn't worth your time If you don't intend to use the information contained in it.

What are you planning to do?

Do you want to be among the top 1% of people who can make things happen? I'm sure you will!

Best of luck!

www.ingramcontent.com/pod-product-compliance
Lightning Source LLC
Chambersburg PA
CBHW071643210326
41597CB00017B/2095